You Must Have Been a Beautiful Baby

THE STARLIGHT STORY

The Starlight Foundation is an international non-profit organization founded in 1982 by actress Emma Samms that helps brighten the lives of seriously ill children ages 4 through 18 years.

Starlight's services include granting special wishes as well as providing entertainment and recreational activities for pediatric patients throughout the United States, United Kingdom, Australia and Canada.

VICKI GOLD LEVI, STEVEN HELLER & SEYMOUR CHWAST

You Must Have Been a Beautiful Baby

BABY PICTURES OF THE STARS

HYPERION

NEW YORK

To my A Team - Adam and Alex - V.G.L.
To Nicolas - S.H.
And to all the babies in the world - S.C.

ACKNOWLEDGMENTS

The authors thank all the participating celebrities, publicists, managers, agents, personal assistants, friends and mothers for their generous support and invaluable assistance. Special thanks to:

Carol Brown, Chief Executive of The Starlight Foundation; Michele Posner, Director of Children's Services of The Starlight Foundation; Trudy Richmond Kaplan, Maryann Kulbus, Kelly Klein, Susan Meredith, Mary Miller, Howard Rubin, Iris Ranier Dart, Pat Connell, Mickey Kaufman, Tom Bodkin, Charles Gay, Holly Jacobs, Sheryl Gordon Martinello, Sharyn Felder, Raoul Felder, Cynthia Stewart, Rachael Clarke, Karen Lippert, Trudy Taylor, Leslie McDonald, Karen LeBlanc, Susan Blutman, Dana Freedman, Brad Cafarelli, Linda Brown, Ron Lieberman, Neal Peters, Vera Stern, Marilyn and Alvin Cooperman, Mary McGinnis, Kim Faulkner, Karin Bacon, Susan McCullough, Mario Casciano, Lisa Klausner, Bob Burton, Mary Anderson, Eric Preven, Michael Pollan, Marianne Visconti, Janelle Sperow, Jeannie Goldfarb, Heidi Schaeffer, Karen Samfilippo, Kalen Gorman, Norma Foerderer, Lynnae Crawford, Jack Rosner, Anita Mueden and Farida Sadik.

Extra special thanks to Roxanne Slimak for her design and production, Kate Egan for her editorial assistance, our editor Victoria Di Stasio, our publisher Bob Miller, and our agent Sarah Jane Freymann.

Dan Rather's photographs from "I Remember" (Little, Brown & Co., 1991)

"You Must Have Been a Beautiful Baby" (Harry Warren, Johnny Mercer)
© 1938 Warner Bros. Inc. (Renewed) All Rights Reserved. Used by Permission.

Library of Congress Cataloging-in-Publication Data
Levi, Vicki Gold.
    You must have been a beautiful baby: baby pictures of the stars/
Vicki Gold Levi, Steven Heller & Seymour Chwast. – 1st ed.
    p. cm.
    ISBN 1-56282-934-3
    1. Celebrities – United States – Portraits. 2. Children – United States – Portraits.
I. Heller, Steven. II. Chwast, Seymour. III. Title.
TR681.F3L47 1992
778.9'25 – dc20   92-15937
                                                                      CIP

FIRST EDITION
10 9 8 7 6 5 4 3 2 1

Celebrity watching has become a national pastime. When we see our personal favorites in the movies, on TV or stage, in the political or sports arena, we tend to imagine that they have always been beautiful, sleek, talented, and endlessly fascinating. We lose sight of the fact that they, like us, started as unknown adorable babies – loved and cherished by their parents and families but probably never imagining that they would grow up to be an idol. What we've tried to capture in this book is that early innocence of baby and childhood before fame and glory would transform the little boy or girl next door into a national treasure. The participating celebrities have generously opened their personal family albums in order to benefit the Starlight Foundation which grants the wishes of seriously ill children. We hope you have as much fun taking this privileged peek as we had putting it together.

Candice Bergen

Age 3

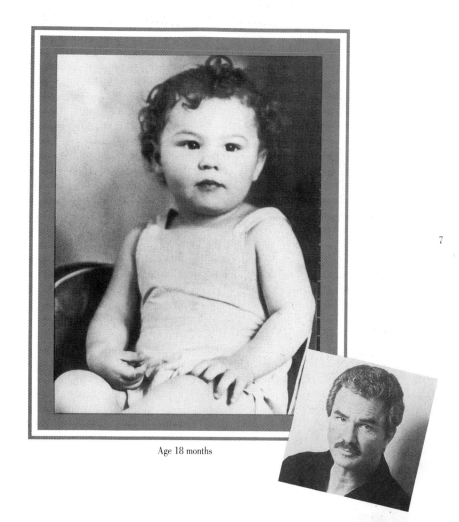

Age 18 months

Calvin Klein

Age 4

Age 2

Paula Abdul

Age 2$^1/_2$ (center) with sister, Wendy, age 9$^1/_2$ (left) and friend

Age 4

Harrison Ford

Age 1

Melanie Griffith
Tippi Hedren

Age 2, Daughter

Age 1 year and 9 months, Mother

Michael J. Fox

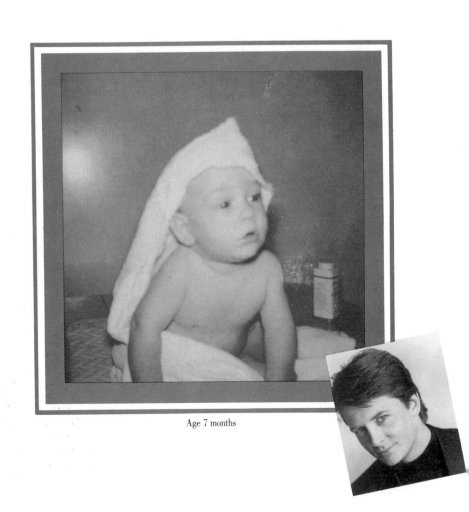

Age 7 months

Age 2

Emma Samms

Age 2

Age 2

Bob Mackie

Age 1$\frac{1}{2}$

Age 13 months

Roger Miller

Age 1

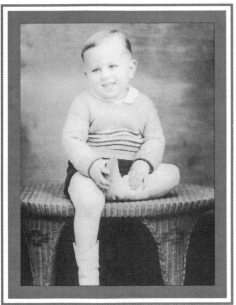

Age 4

Age 3

Kathie Lee Gifford

Age 4 months

Age 11 months

Billy Joel

Age 1

Age 3 months

Jackie Mason

Age 7 months

Age 1¹/₂

Howie Mandel
Debbie Gibson

Age 9 months

28

Age 2

Age 14 months

Phil Donahue

Age 3

Age 3

Peter Allen

Age 3

Age 2$^1/_2$

Joan Rivers

Age 4

Age 2 ½

Dave Winfield

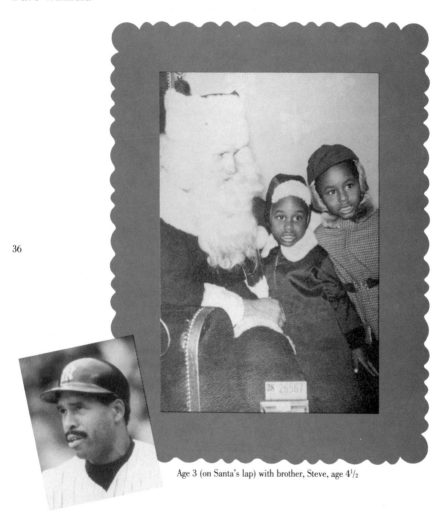

Age 3 (on Santa's lap) with brother, Steve, age 4$^1/_2$

Martha Quinn
Hulk Hogan

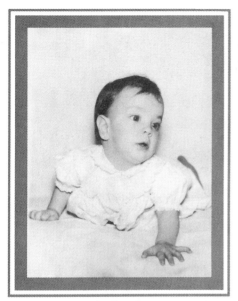

Age 4 months

37

Age 3

Stephen Nichols

Age 2 and sister, Penny, age 4¹/₂

Age 2

Judge Reinhold

Age 3 months

Age 3

Tatum O'Neal

Age 5 months

John McEnroe, Jr.

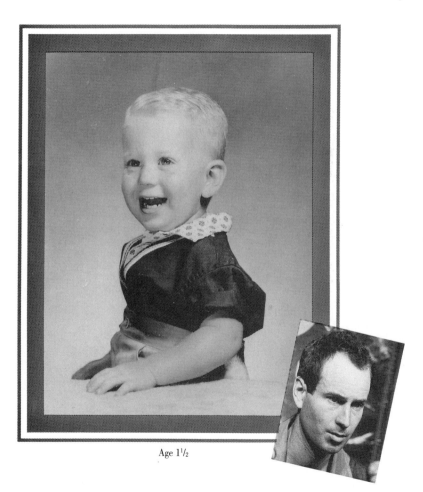

43

Age 1¹/₂

Kevin Bacon
Aidan Quinn

Age 3

Age 6 months and mother, Teresa

Age 6 weeks

Gerardo

Age 4

Age 3¹/₂ with father, Joseph

Lily Tomlin

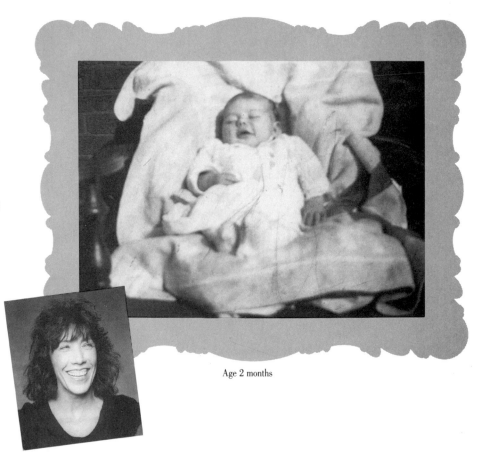

Age 2 months

Age 4

Dan Rather

Age 3 months with mother, Byrl

Age 3 with brother, Paul, age 2

Wendy Wilson
Carnie Wilson

52

Age 9 months

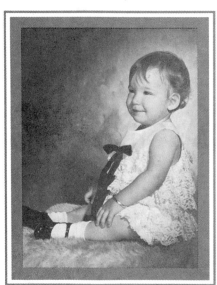

Age 2½

Carnie, Wendy and Chynna of Wilson Phillips

Age 3, Daughter

Age 1, Mother

Mary Hart

54

Age 3

Age 2

Barbara Mandrell

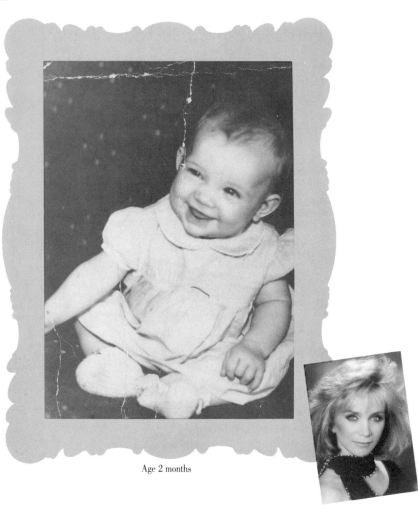

Age 2 months

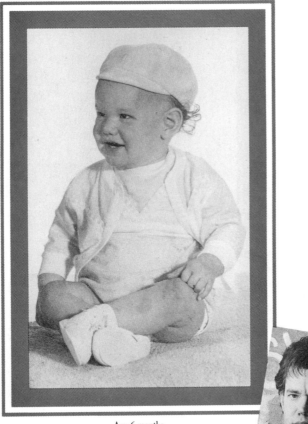

Age 6 months

Isaac Stern

Age 1

Age $3^1/_2$

Betty Comden

Age 3 with brother, Nathaniel, age 6

Phyllis Newman
Adolph Green

Age 3

61

Age 4 months

Susan Lucci

Age 11 months

Jean-Claude Van Damme

63

Age 1

Kirk Cameron

Age 8 months

Age 10 months

Yoko Ono

Age 4

Age 6 months with mother, June

Steve Garvey
Mary Frann

Age 1

Age 3

68

Age 5 months

Natalie Cole

Age 3½

Age 3

Anthony Quinn

Age 4, with sister, Stella, age 2

Tyne Daly

73

Age 3

Angie Dickinson

Age 3¹/₂

Age 4

With son and wife

Age 3 (on lap) with mother, Mary, and brother, Elmo, age 8

Danny Wood
Joseph McIntyre

Age 2 with sisters Pamela age 5, Melissa age 6 and Bethany age 7

New Kids on the Block

Age 3

Sally Jessy Raphaël

Age 3

Maury Povich

Age 1¹/₂

79

A. Martinez

Age 7 months

Age 3

Zubin Mehta

Age 3

Olympia Dukakis

Age 1

Lesley Gore

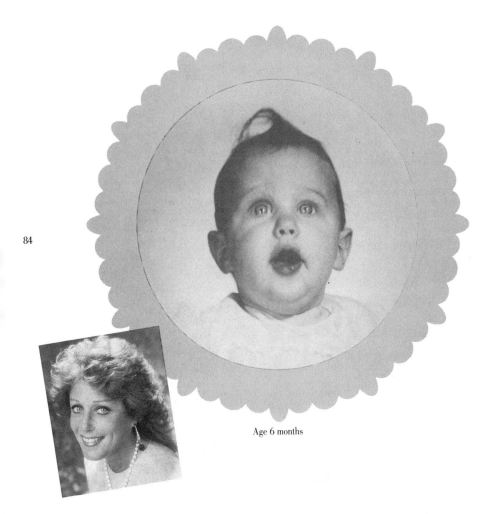

Age 6 months

Dick Clark
Ed McMahon

Age 6 months

85

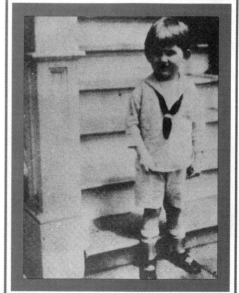

Age 3

Age 2 (left) with brother, Lloyd, age 1

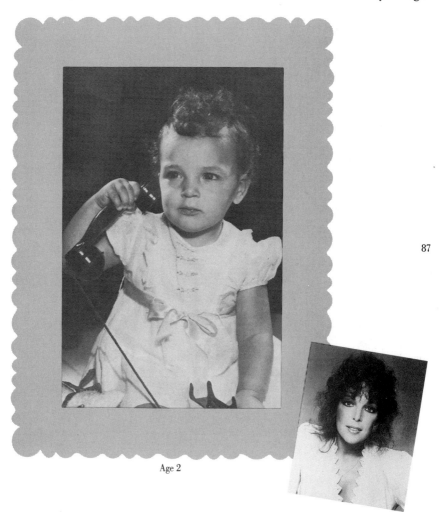

Age 2

Hugh Hefner

Age 18 months

Age 18 months

Edward Asner

Age 3

Age 8 months

William F. Buckley, Jr.

Age 4

Age 2

Age 4

Pat Boone

Age 3 months

Age 6 months

The authors express thanks to the participating
celebrities who provided the baby and current
photographs for this book. We would also like to thank
the following photographers whose work appears in this
book and are listed on the pages below and we apologize
to those whose photographs are not credited.

CURRENT PHOTOGRAPHS ONLY

Baz, Michael, 43

Boyar, Rick, 56

Burton, Christina, 61 (bottom)

Caravaglia,Tom, 90

Crum, Lee, 71

Edgeworth, Anthony, 50

Exley, Jonathon, 16, 39

Fischella, Russ, 13 (bottom)

Frank, Kathleen A./ © 1991, Miss America Pageant, 65

Goldsmith, Lynn, 77 (2 headshots)

Gorman, Greg, 41

Granitz, Steve, 47

Hurrell, George, 70

Kredenser, Peter, 93 (top)

Langdon, Harry, 33, 87

Leibovitz, Annie, 23

Prigent, Roger, 66

Putnam, Don, 20

Scheinmann, David, 67

St. Nicholas, Randee, 32, 54, 55

Taylor, Steve, 37 (bottom)

Tighe, Mike, 44 (bottom)

Tolot, Alberto, 10, 52

© 1991 Capital Cities/ ABC, Inc., 62

© 1991 Morgan Creek Productions, Inc., 49

© 1991 Paramount Pictures Corporation, 79

© 1990 Universal City Studios, Inc., 44 (top)